BOOKS
DO
FURNISH
A
ROOM

BOOKS
DO
FURNISH
A
ROOM

Leslie Geddes-Brown

MERRELL
LONDON · NEW YORK

ROOM 606

INTRODUCTION

This library in Costa Rica won Gianni Botsford the Lubetkin Prize for architecture in 2008. He designed it for his father, the journalist and academic Keith Botsford. The shelves, and indeed the outer structure of the building itself, are raised on wooden stilts in order to protect the library of 17,000 books from the humid climate and prevent attacks by termites.

Although writers like to believe that books have a higher, sterner purpose, nonetheless, they also *do* furnish a room. Take an unadorned space, cover one wall with crowded bookshelves, add a chair and a table, also crowded with books, and you have a furnished room.

It might even be a good-looking room, although, to judge by the rooms of famous authors – currently featured weekly in a major national newspaper – this is rarely the case. A glance at the room where one such apparently otherwise highly civilized writer works reveals that the curtains, unchanged since a previous occupant, dangle unhooked and the books stagger in heaps. Another writer has filled her window – the room's only light source – with toppling piles of shabby books, unintentionally creating an effect more akin to being in a prison basement.

So, books do furnish a room – but not always very well. This book, with images from stylish houses, taken by world-famous photographers, intends to show how it can be done.

Private libraries are emphatically not public libraries. That is, they do not need the Dewey system, as devised by the American librarian Melvil Dewey (ten main classifications divided into one hundred numbers, with decimal subdivisions for further subcategories). Since the only people who are going to use these libraries are you, your family and friends, the classification can be as eccentric as you wish, as long

as you all understand it. All books with red covers together, for example, or anything to do with horses, whether racing or Stubbs paintings. If the system works well enough, that's all that's needed.

Resign yourself, however: whatever system you adopt, it will not be perfect (even under the Dewey system, books get misplaced), and all readers must accustom themselves to endless searches for that elusive book that has a dark-green cover – which turns out to be scarlet. You may never find what you are looking for, but, on the other hand, some long-lost book may surface during the search.

Imagine what it was like when books were written on clay tablets, more than 5000 years ago in Mesopotamia: not much fun to consult. Or consider the papyrus scrolls, which had titles inscribed on wooden tags, in the great library of Alexandria in 300 BC. The aim there was to collect every book in the world, which, even at that date, amounted to 750,000 volumes. They were amassed in pigeonholes, which is roughly what we do today with books on bookshelves. When much of the library was shipped to Rome by Julius Caesar in 48 BC, books were stacked against the walls with tables provided for reading. Other libraries, surprisingly, were attached to bathhouses.

Before the invention of printing by Johannes Gutenberg in Germany in about 1439, readers had variously to cope with wooden boards packed flat on shelves, and inscribed parchment scrolls made from untanned, treated cattle skins, a material that was deeply resistant to being folded – or unfolded.

By AD 600 monasteries had come up with inter-library loans, and public libraries were opened in France in 1367; the Vatican and the University of Oxford opened libraries

How eccentric can you get? The designer and builder Sallie Trout has created her own library by enclosing bookshelves within the central staircase of her new home. She reaches the books via a bosun's chair that is fastened to a chain hoist, hung from the ceiling above. Or she can use the stairs.

in the 1400s. America's oldest library, at Harvard, was opened in 1638, followed by the German State Library in Berlin in 1661.

Such historic libraries were certainly conscious of the beauty of books, which were treated in a manner befitting their status as expensive luxuries. Bookshelves were ornately carved in the finest of woods, the floors were of intricate marble, and ceilings were decorated with plasterwork or frescoes.

While the modern public library hardly comes up to these standards, often being filled equally with tattered books and eccentric people keeping warm, private libraries can be as formal and carefully designed as the Vatican's. I know of one, in a converted electricity substation with handsome curved walls, that consciously emulates the London Library with its semi-transparent floors made of iron grilles, and bookshelves on two storeys; and when I visited Holkham Hall, in Norfolk, the Earl of Leicester had a librarian on his private staff to organize the eighteenth-century library that had been created when the house was built.

Provided that you have enough books, it's not difficult to create a proper library in this formal mode: you simply line with neat shelves most of the walls of a room of whatever size you can afford, and fill them. Add a smart desk with comfortable chair alongside and, if there is any

wall space left, a series of prints or paintings. The room is now a library. This space need not be devoted simply to reading: with a round table in the centre, it can double as a dining-room. There are few places more romantic for a candle-lit dinner à *deux* than a book-clad room. Similarly, if you are lucky enough to have a generous entrance or stairway hall, the space can also act as a library. Even unconsidered areas, beneath windows, over picture rails and under the stairs, can be converted into libraries.

But for a library to work well, attention to detail is necessary. The way to make the best of any space is to ensure that the shelves are the right height for the books that you have, and that at least 5 centimetres (2 inches) are allowed above each book. This enables you to pull any volume out easily and without damage. Good lighting is essential, so that titles are visible at all times. There should be handy shelves or tables near by where you can pile or read the books you remove.

Of course, not everyone is a serious reader or researcher, and not everyone actually wants a library. Volumes in decorative bookcases – antique, designer-led or home-made – can be spread about the house in small batches. Every spare bedroom needs a small rack of books at the least, and most of us need space for recipe books in the kitchen. Indeed, splitting up books by subject and keeping them where they will be most needed is one of the simplest forms of classification. So, short stories in the spare room; miscellanies to be dipped into in the bathroom; recipe books in the kitchen; and coffee-table books, obviously, consigned to the coffee table or to a special table in the living-room. You might add books with fine bindings to a formal dining-room, and a pile of dog-eared paperbacks to your own bedroom. Atlases and maps go in

the hall, if there is space for them, and gardening books on shelves near the back door and its wellington boots.

In schemes where the books are truly there only as furniture, the spines can be chosen for their decorative value – though, obviously, gilt-and-leather bindings tend to the fusty and formal, while rows of dictionaries and encyclopedias are solemnly virtuous. Any old rubbish can be disguised with a plain paper cover, or there's fun to be had with decorative handmade jackets – marbled papers or wallpaper, say, or even covers made from exotic newspapers, such as Chinese or Russian ones. If the books are valueless, conservation issues don't apply.

If, however, each book is worth a tidy sum – you'd be surprised at the value of even twenty-year-old first editions – then store them tidily on shelves, neither crammed in nor so loosely that they're keeling over. Keep an eye out for bookworms (silverfish rather than studious children), which eat paper and glue, and try to keep humidity both low and constant. If your tomes are so valuable (or rude) that they need to be kept behind locked doors, the humidity level is even more important, as gentle draughts are a great help in conservation. Books kept behind closed doors may need an occasional airing.

The value of a book tends to increase with lack of handling, pristine being best, and dog-eared and crumbling, unsurprisingly, being worst. Ideally, recipe books should not get too bespattered with tomato ketchup; garden guides should be left indoors, and first editions by the likes of J.K. Rowling should, unfortunately, not be read – their covers should remain intact. I suppose slip covers are helpful here, but they are a particular dislike of mine, invented, I think, by publishers to increase the cover price.

But it's a sad world where the intrinsic value of a book is more important than what it has to say. Although I would never scribble notes in the margins of books (however tempted I am as a proof-reader), I do value the marginal notes of others: the dedications and birthday greetings on the fly-leaf, and the occasional shopping list, newspaper article or pressed flower that drops from the pages of a second-hand book. They are mementoes of previous readers whose libraries have been dispersed for the benefit of others.

And, yes, libraries should be dispersed. There is nothing more depressing than a fossilized set of bookshelves, over-provided with Holy Bibles and sermons written by nineteenth-century divines, which have not been pored over for a century. Libraries, like all rooms, can become dated.

So, while many authors treat books with disdain (and disapprove of books furnishing a room), the jumble of volumes by a writer's desk, the way books are used to prop up uneven desk legs or signal dangerous holes in a carpet, are far better than treating them with a conservator's cotton gloves.

Books are there to be read – and to furnish a room.

LIVING WITH BOOKS

In my view, there should be books in every room of the house, with the possible exception of the larder. Books in the attic waiting to be reread; in the garage, waiting to be recycled at the jumble sale; and, of course, in piles in the box room. These are just in store, awaiting their moment. All other rooms also need their quota, ready to be pulled from the shelf or the coffee table for a desultory browse. You never know when you might need a quick fix – for books are as addictive as any class A drug. Those lucky enough to have the habit cannot go without reading-matter for even a day.

The books you live with are not the same as those you work with. Books in living-rooms and bedrooms are for pleasure rather than study. They won't tell you the capital of Burkina (Ouagadougou) or how to rid roses of blackfly, but they will change your mood, or satisfy it.

To me a room without books is missing an essential feature, as important as lights, chairs or carpets. Or pictures: in their way, books are like pictures on the wall; they reveal whether you are a minimalist with all covers hidden under plain wrappers, a maximalist whose every room has a generously filled bookcase, or an anarchist whose preferred method of storage is an untidy heap. Amateur detectives in the whodunnits I read (ready in piles by bed and bath) often detect the reality behind the characters in the story by a quick look at the bookshelves: a shelf devoted to undetectable poisons may be a bad sign (or good, depending), as are heavy devotional works, useful for bashing enemies over the head. When I visit friends' houses, it's always heartening to see a few bodice-rippers and thrillers in among the Booker Prize-winners.

The careful host will make sure that guests have what they want: short stories in the spare bedroom for brief visits; luscious illustrated books on the coffee table for aspirationalists; and a few jokers, such as *Winnie-the-Pooh* in Latin or the complete *Encyclopædia Britannica* from the 1880s, which will help solve arguments over dinner – and those heavy red volumes are totally in keeping with dining-room decor. Children's rooms are, of course, full of the best writing, so you can drop in from time to time for a discreet dose of Dahl or J.K. without betraying how much you love their supposedly 'childish' stories.

I collect, among others, cookery books, and my kitchen cupboards groan with them. On one occasion I found some outside caterers enjoying a literary feast while preparing a real feast for a party. Book dealers suggest that such books should not be splashed with soup. What do they know about it?

Living-rooms

The two niches beside a living-room fire make a very good starting point for bookshelves, in that the space is already there. A few neat shelves, perhaps with some architectural detail to them, such as trim capitals or reeded uprights, add permanency to the structure. It's good sense, too, to make the shelves line up with the fireplace wall, even if it makes them overly deep. It's just neater.

If your living-room is very large, an oversized set of bookshelves will reduce the space and add warmth to the whole. When the prevailing decor is casual, cottagey or comfortable, the books can echo this by not being too rigorously organized. And, of course, in a formal room, whether high Georgian or minimalist, the opposite principle applies.

Living-room books should be less for work and reference and more for casual reading, if you have space to make these distinctions. Also, mixing books with decorative pieces – whether prints, or casts of Greek philosophers, casually levered between volumes – always looks good in a living-room. The aim is to be inviting.

◥ Suzy Murphy, an artist, has raised the height of her bookshelves in a London town house to give the room an overall spaciousness. The painting, *Moroccan Tea*, is by Emma McClure.

▶ The library-cum-dressing-room in the New York apartment of Amy Fine Collins includes artwork by Robert Couturier, Gene Mayer, Karl Lagerfeld and Victor Skrebneski.

▶▶ Libraries don't come much grander than this one, which is in Mellerstain in Scotland and was designed by Robert Adam in the early 1770s. The paintings are by Zucci. Despite the grandeur, the sofas, chairs and burning fire create an atmosphere of comfortable warmth.

Previous pages: The Paris living-room of architect and designer Jean Oddes is a thoughtful mixture of ancient and modern. The bookshelves are sparse and metallic but covered with diamond-patterned wire. The urns on the upper shelves are echoed by colossal prints of Classical urns on either side.

▲ Shelves of books in a darkened corridor lead to a sunlit study in designer Suzanne Boyd's New York apartment. The textile is a logger's tent.

◄ The two shades of green – olive and emerald – are an unusual combination in Patrice Butler's London study, but, combined with Classical pillars and floor-to-ceiling bookcases, they create a room of elegant formality.

▲ Despite the apparently relaxed way in which the books in this room are arranged, their owner, the famous artist Sandro Chia, ensures that he can find any book easily: each one is numbered. In front of the bookcases is an eighteenth-century sofa, with one of Chia's paintings propped against its back. The old terracotta tiles give away the Tuscan origin of the castle.

▲ Arne Maynard, the garden designer, deliberately chose comfortable furniture to complement his country house in Lincolnshire, England. The whole was designed to be informal and rural in feeling. The bookshelves are built in on the wall facing the fireplace.

◣ This Georgian house in Wales has, too, been designed to look as though a family has lived there for generations. Stuffed birds in glass cases surmount the old volumes in the bookshelves, adding a touch of apparently authentic history to the room.

▼ Here, the atmosphere in a new barn in Johannesburg, by architect Karen Wygers of Urban Solutions, creates a feeling of history in a modern room. The symmetrical arrangement of bookshelves, easy chairs and pictures is very much in the eighteenth-century tradition. The designer was Julia Twigg.

The bookshelves in designer
Frédéric Méchiche's Paris
apartment are deliberately untidy,
contrasting with the order of
the room and the formal
arrangement of chairs and sofa
centred on the fire. The panelling
and floor were salvaged.

Salvaged wood was used here,
too, to create symmetrical
bookcases to complement the
beams of this country house in
upstate New York. The brick walls
were also deliberately left shabby
by design company Irvine,
Fleming, Bell to increase the
room's rustic appearance.

Bedrooms

◤ Richard Rogers designed this two-storey glass penthouse on top of a Victorian warehouse. The bedroom is part of the open-plan living-space, which can be sectioned off by sliding walls.

▼ Most avid readers like to keep bookshelves handy in every room of the house. This is the former bedroom of English designer Nina Campbell. Shelves have been inserted in the space beside the window of her west London flat.

There should be a distinction between the books suitable for a guest bedroom and those for your own lair. Guests should be offered a mixture of dates and styles, with an emphasis on short reads (so they don't take the books home). The shelves could be small in number, so as not to be too threatening, and the volumes themselves just a bit dog-eared and well read. The aim is to enable your guests to tell at a glance that the reading-matter is definitely for them. Small, movable, antique shelves for only a dozen or so books, or a pair of entertaining bookends, are just right. So are those revolving bookcases that are free-standing or would work as bedside tables.

Your own bedroom is another matter. Depending on how addicted you are to the literary life, storage can vary from a small, ever-changing pile by the bed to a bedroom entirely furnished with shelves, as if one were going to bed in a library, surrounded by old friends. Otherwise, custom-made shelves work well between Georgian windows, while shelves once intended for hats or boots can be piled with paperbacks. In either case, really good bedside lighting, such as wall lights beside the bed or Anglepoise-type lamps on bedside tables, is crucial.

▼ Books divide as much as
they unite a couple. On one
side of this bed are architectural
books used by architect John
Comparelli, in case he needs
a touch of Palladio in the night.
On the other bedside are his
wife, Lucy's, less-organized
objects, with books on the
higher shelves. This is their
home in east London.

Richard Howard's book-filled apartment in New York is also featured later, as an example of an extreme bibliophile's lair (pages 66–67). Every wall is filled with book-crammed shelves, so hats have to hang on doors, and pictures on door jambs.

A glance reveals that this is an architect's bedroom – in fact, Hugh Newell Jacobsen's, in a restored Nantucket barn. The furnishings and colour are minimal and the books confined to strict cubes along one wall.

◄ A library in a log cabin in Kenya was constructed by the artist Timothy Brooke. The cabin's frame is made of cypress fixed to a cement base and clad in cedar planks. Books find themselves neighbours with hiking boots and fishing floats.

◤ Large books are often better displayed horizontally rather than vertically – although it makes them harder to pull out. These are in the master bedroom of the designer Miv Watts, in her former Norfolk cottage.

▼ Many designers have more magazines than books to store. This is the case in James Andrew's small New York apartment. The custom-built bookcases create a formal bedroom for the interior designer.

Children's spaces

I don't believe books are going to become obsolete in the foreseeable future, so it's important to get children reading as early as possible, if only to counter the temptations of computer games. Books in children's rooms also add a touch of civilization where it may be desperately needed.

Most children's rooms tend to be decorated with simplicity and in primary colours. Fortunately, most children's books are also jacketed in primary colours and are small enough for little hands to hold. It's up to parents to make the room inviting, while encouraging toddler tidiness by having special areas designated for books. These can be shelves handily arranged beside the bed; a small, mobile bookshelf on a bedside table; or books arranged along with toys, making both into decorative features. Teddy can be used to prop up a row of books, or a series of atlases can be placed next to a globe.

Another idea is to use a robust basket for holding books in progress beside the bed, so that there's always something to hand on light mornings. I do think books and reading should be made into an enjoyable hobby as soon as children can read, thereby encouraging them – who knows? – to become the owners of fine libraries in the future.

Nicolas Barker is a publisher, so it was in his interest to get his children dedicated early to books and reading. Their favourites are all stored within easy reach in the family's west London home.

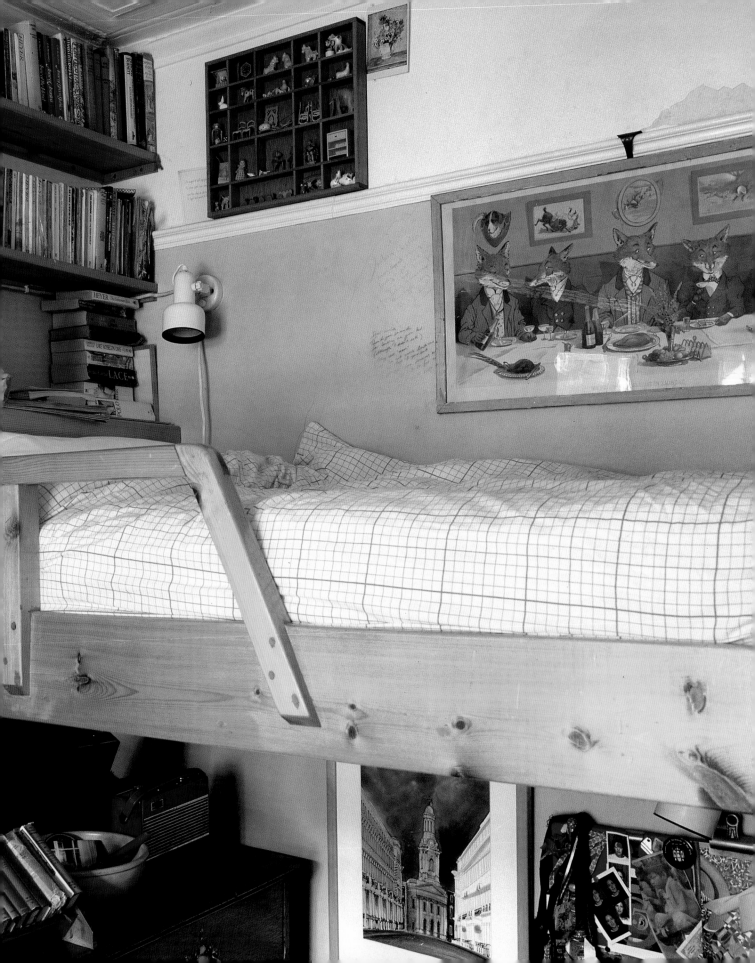

◀ In Jon and Sasha Dorey's home in south-west England, a bunk bed is designed with shelf space at the end to provide useful storage for family books. These slip neatly under the bed's ladder.

▶ Children are much more likely to enjoy reading if books feature from early on in their rooms. In this room designed by Heather Luke in a house on England's Sussex Downs, the shelves are as friendly as the soft toys on the beds.

Living with books

Johnny Grey added a children's
play area to the basement kitchen
of a large Victorian terraced
house in London. Not only are
the geometric cube doors
attractive, but they also hide
a lot of less good-looking
toys and books.

Kitchens

If, like me, you are a collector of recipe books
(and it's hard not to be, so beguiling are they today),
then you will want special shelves for them – or at
least for those most often in use – in the kitchen. My
solution is to stack them in a large Victorian kitchen
cupboard that has doors. For – contrary to my
philosophy in many other rooms – I think it's sensible
to protect your cookery books from the steam and
grease that cooking can create. Nonetheless, I like
my cookery books to look well used rather than
so neat and untouched that it's obvious I never
open them.

I reckon you need space for a good dozen
favourite recipe books that are used at least once a
month, though more probably once a week. If kitchen
space is tight, other titles, dealing with seasonal food
or cuisine from a specific country, can be stored
elsewhere and brought in when needed. If shelf space
is crammed with pans and crockery, the books can
be piled alongside or even interspersed with the more
decorative china.

If your kitchen is a farmhouse one, then don't
stick to recipe books alone; have friendly novels,
biographies and children's books piled by the old
sofa or comfortable chair, for those moments when
you're waiting for the potatoes to boil. It's called
multi-tasking.

Cookery-book fanatics, such
as me, need generous shelves
in the kitchen (although this is
not the place to keep valuable
first editions). This Bermudian
kitchen keeps crockery behind
glass doors alongside a shelf
for plenty of recipe books.

▼◢ Bibliophiles just can't help collecting, even if their compulsion means that they eventually find themselves being driven from the house by piles of books. These busy shelves belong to Joan Vass, the art historian and ex-curator of the Museum of Modern Art in New York. She has mixed together kitchenware, crockery, recipe books and volumes on the history of food and drink wherever space allows.

▲ Every grand yacht – even those on shore – needs a stash of books. An overhead bookshelf has been built into Jon and Sasha Dorey's seaside home, which is decorated with lifebelts and other nautical impedimenta.

Bathrooms

Bathrooms, with all that steam about, are not exactly conducive to maintaining books in peak condition. But who wants to keep first editions and illustrated manuscripts by the bath? What the bathroom reader likes is something to entertain while (let's be honest here) he or she is on the lavatory. Bathrooms and lavatories are fine and private places to indulge in a little light reading.

As a child, I would vanish to our Victorian lav, which had a fine mahogany seat covering the entire width of the room, simply to read. The charm of reading in the bathroom is all about self-indulgence and privacy.

At the very least you need piles of paperbacks to flip through; short stories are good, as are those guides to astrology or cinema that come free with newspapers. Otherwise, a proper bookshelf with mixed reading for all tastes or, in large bathrooms, a free-standing antique bookcase, work well. Indeed, this size of bathroom can be arranged like a living-room, with free-standing shelves and even a fire. If, conversely, space is too short for even the smallest paperback shelf, arrange one just outside the door as a welcome.

Although not ideal for book conservation, bathrooms are places to contemplate life and read all about it. Axel Vervoordt's castle outside Antwerp contains a secret door, lined with false books, which leads into a marble-clad bathroom with an adjoining set of real bookshelves.

▲ Many top fashion designers take inspiration from the arts of the past. This small stack of books is in Karl Lagerfeld's studio in Rome. The bathroom has walls painted to look like wood, and a spiral staircase that leads to the main bedroom.

Some of us just can't help collecting, which leads to some very unlikely rooms. This bathroom, crowded with an improbable combination of stuffed birds and books, belonged to Lord McAlpine at West Green in Somerset, England. The house is now in the keeping of the National Trust.

In this panelled bathroom
in Eastnor Castle, Herefordshire,
built-in bookshelves are ranged
alongside a fireplace and
family prints.

Living with books

▼ Where better to relax than in a bath with a book? This natty bookrest is fixed beside the taps in the bathroom of a publisher (of course) – Nicolas Barker. Take care, however, not to expose valuable books to the steam treatment.

▲ The same publisher ensures that the loo in his west London house has plenty of shelves for books. Penguins and other small paperbacks find a perfect home.

Corridors, hallways and landings

In most houses, especially old ones, there is generous space in the corridors and landings – space that has no real purpose. So why not use it to hold your books? This will not only insulate the areas concerned (books do insulate a room), but also make them far more interesting.

There are many very different ways in which to make use of forgotten corners. Many landings and wide corridors can easily accommodate a full floor-to-ceiling set of bookshelves. This will cut only a foot or so off the space, especially if you choose to limit the books to those that are smaller sizes, leaving larger ones for the main rooms. But if space is still limited, books can be perched on single shelves or combined with other ornaments so that the effect is less formal.

In using halls, corridors and landings, it's worth trying to limit the books to a certain type. They could all be dictionaries – of biography, French, quotations – so that you know where to find them. They could be simply paperbacks, perhaps arranged by genre or alphabet; or, if you have special interests – such as vintage cars, Chinese furniture or genealogy – these books can be isolated in their special shelves.

A modern series of bookshelves, painted white, looks quite at ease with the rough wooden banisters of the French farmhouse belonging to designers Bella and Giles Gibb. Landings are often spacious enough to have a foot lopped off them to make room for shelves.

▲ Unsurprisingly, publisher
Nicolas Barker has a feeling for
books (see his bathroom and loo
earlier, page 45). Here, in his
west London home, books mass
all the way up several staircases.
The effect is tidy, thanks to
careful sizing of the shelves
to fit the books.

▶ A reeded, built-in bookcase,
painted a deep jade, is in perfect
keeping with the English
country-house look. A matching
curtain to the side lends cohesion
to the scheme created by the
designer Mikaela Irwin, while
pottery lions serve as bookends.

◄ This effective library was once the foreman's office in an old carpenters' workshop in Paris. Antiques dealer Mony Linz Einstein has teamed distressed shelves with panelling and a plain wooden floor.

▼ A neat set of shelves is built in beside a door to the garden in this Long Island home, designed by the architectural firm Cicognani Kalla. The glass door lets in light that shines on the decorative spines.

▼ A stable door gives away the origin of this comfortable English home designed by Norwegian architect Vilhemm Koren. In this case, the books are deliberately given plenty of head room.

◄ Offices and studies look smarter and are better organized if files and ugly books are arranged in standard box files, here interspersed with books. In this vaulted Roman flat, the deep chest of drawers holds antique maps.

► A deep dado rail has been put to use as a running bookshelf in this Dublin town house. The strong colour scheme holds the area together and creates a streamlined effect that prevents the open shelves from appearing untidy.

WORKING
WITH
BOOKS

It's a dull library or study where every book can always be found, although all of us who work with books need some kind of system. Most writers I've talked to group their books by subject rather than alphabetically, but most have also had to evolve more complex solutions. For a start, books come in a huge variety of sizes: not only height and width, but also depth, and this means that shelves have to be graded; deep books go under the breakfront and large tomes in a special big-book stack, while paperbacks and classic editions generally perch on small shelves. So, to make the best use of space, the perfect system must be amended.

Next, there is the question of use: some books may be left for decades until the perfect moment arrives (I have a collection of car-auction catalogues that was useless until I needed to identify a 1911 De Dion Bouton in an early photograph). These can be stashed up impossible heights, reached only with a ladder. Similarly, the largest books can be at ground level, giving the groaning upper shelves a bit of relief.

But, then again, I want my library or study to look good. This is done by massing together books of similar bindings. Early Book Club ones, bound in buckram with neat leather labels on the spine, are one example, as are early Penguins in orange, green or turquoise livery.

Everyman produces fine-looking classics, as do paperback publishers Persephone and Virago. Group these together for looks and you will always know where to find them. Similarly, runs of encyclopedias, blue-bound Oxford University Press reference manuals, or other publications with a firm identity will give the library shelves a sense of cohesion, a basis for the wilder combinations that exist elsewhere.

On the subject of order and systems, finally, I do like a little anarchy in the library. Searching for that vital book can lead to other discoveries; books long vanished that you had forgotten. This is always a treat.

Should you keep your books behind glass? That's a matter of personal choice, partly determined by the books' age and value (some books can be surprisingly valuable: my *Big Red Book of Tomatoes* [1999] by Lindsay Bareham is worth more than £100). Glass protects from dust, but is rather depressing, for it shows that the books are not often read but treated too preciously. My feeling, also, is that glass encourages conditions harmful to books, such as humidity. Great libraries, such as the London Library, that at York Minster and those in the imposing statelies, don't bother with glass. What's wrong with just picking out the reference book and blowing the dust from its pages?

The formal library

It is rare to find a modern library that is designed to be formal; most formal libraries were established in the eighteenth or nineteenth centuries, when the rich had time to read books and reading was in the ascendant. Added to this was the fact that publishers as we know them did not exist. Your books were bound in such a way as to suit you and your library, often in leather (morocco) or at least with leather spines and corners. Each library would have its own style of binding, which resulted in shelves full of books sporting similar-coloured leathers and typefaces on their spines. Furthermore, since books were hand set and valuable, libraries formed an important part of the house. The decor – painted ceilings, tapestries, ornately carved shelves – echoed this status, as did the size and position of the room in the house.

Some libraries today imitate such conscious grandeur, using custom-made shelves, numbered stacks, upper-floor balconies and matching desks for serious reading. These are for committed bibliophiles who venerate books and enjoy hours spent with them in inspiring comfort. Many of these libraries go so far as to get books specially bound, or at least to collect works that have old-fashioned leather and buckram covers. These formal spaces also have their own accessories – in particular, library steps or ladders in antique mahogany, as well as lecterns.

The perfect English country-house formal library, at Eastnor Castle in Herefordshire, a late Georgian house decorated, later, by Pugin. The Amritsar carpet was made specially for this grand space, while the six tapestries by Philippe de Maecht, woven in Paris in about 1615, show scenes from the myth of Andromeda. The books have been clearly bound by successive owners in complementary bindings.

The formal library

The only colour in this cool, white room is provided by two walls of books, tailored to surround the window. The room, designed by architect Hugh Newell Jacobsen, is part of a Nantucket barn that dates from the 1840s.

Working with books

▲ This cool, book-lined corridor is in Elghammar, Sweden's great Palladian house. The architect was Giacomo Quarenghi, who was based in St Petersburg. The library was originally situated elsewhere in the house, and was moved to this corridor, known as the Small Gallery, in the nineteenth century.

▲ Rough, untreated wood makes Brutalist bookshelves in this double-height library in a country house in upstate New York. The designer was Irvine, Fleming, Bell. Minimal but effective lights at the top of the bookcases enable titles to be easily read.

▶ Inside the boundaries of Imperial Rome, this flat is owned by an art historian, and was restored by the architect Raimondo Pento. Cohesion is given to the books by the line of volumes in standardized bindings on the top shelf.

Working with books

◄ The owner of this library at the Castello di Massino near Turin clearly decided that looks should take precedence over practicality, as all the books here are arranged by size rather than author or subject. The bindings, too, are standardized, creating a sense of calm and order in the two rooms.

▲ At the centre of the room that can be seen through the doorway is a circular bookcase flooded with light. The library was probably created around 1670 and is listed in an inventory of 1736.

The informal library

The main difference between the formal and informal library is that the latter relies far less on traditional bindings to give the shelves coherence. Informal the shelves may appear, but they are often laid out with as much care – though less grandeur – than the magnificent rooms of grand houses, museums and palaces. Libraries are rooms dedicated to books and, even if casual in appearance, informal libraries use books to cover every available wall, floor to ceiling. Some may achieve extra shelving by being laid out in bays so that the bookcases not only cover all the walls but also jut out into the room. This adds many feet of book space and allows the room, if large, to be divided into areas with desks for study, or relaxed spaces for reading on a sofa or easy chair.

In such libraries, books tend to be less regimented, being stacked horizontally as well as vertically in order to accommodate extra-large sizes. Spaces left above rows of books are packed with more volumes tucked in horizontally. Books used for work in progress lie about in piles on desks or on the floor. Such informal libraries are serious places that also manage to be delightfully cluttered and friendly.

When you have 12,000 books to store, as architect Randolph Martz does, you need to use up every space. This is his draughting-room in his New Orleans home. A sense of order and formality is created by keeping behind glass the books that are in the tall cases.

◄ A Belgian art collector enlivens an otherwise somewhat staid library by adding a compressed plastic sculpture by New Realist Cesar in the central space. This draws the eye away from the chaotic shelves.

◄ You'd never guess that this was the library of the French shoe designer Christian Louboutin (he of the red soles). The original stonework and hexagonal terracotta tiles of the French country house have been complemented by an understated yet fairly formal arrangement.

Overleaf: Bibliophilia reaches a peak in Richard Howard's New York home (see also pages 28–29). The poet and translator has made his entire space into one enormous library. The shelves are carefully constructed to fit the varying sizes of the books, which provide good insulation, too.

The study

If I have to make a distinction between a library and a study, it would be that desks and other workspaces are as important in the whole study as the books in it, whereas libraries are devoted to books. Studies are where work is done at a busy desk in a comfortable chair; books for the work in progress may be brought in specially rather than stacked all around the room. I use an old-fashioned mahogany trolley on which to pile books that I need for an ongoing chapter. It makes it easier to concentrate on the subject than if one is surrounded by so much else.

Studies come in all styles from the monastic – aged chestnut writing-desk, brass candlesticks as seen in Renaissance paintings – to the starkly modern, where everything is hidden behind closed, handleless cupboard doors. Think, on the one hand, of Vita Sackville-West's study in her Tudor tower at Sissinghurst, Kent; and, on the other, of a John Pawson all-white minimalist workroom. Studies can also be tiny, shoe-horned into a landing with a single bookcase, or eased into a box room that at least provides privacy. But each needs to be in the character of its owner, a place where the student can concentrate best.

◥ You can tell this is an office designed from scratch by architects – in this case Project Orange, working on a new house in Suffolk, England. The shelves are divided into rectangles, stacked like bricks in a wall, and the space behind each rectangle is of a different colour. The desk is integrated into the whole.

▶ The interior designer John Stefanidis has with typical grace solved the problem of this study's sloping ceilings. The books are stacked in columns around the door, but so neatly that the slope above is unobtrusive. Stefanidis's country retreat was created from a series of converted cow byres.

When space is short, the most
surprising rooms can be pressed
into service for storing books.
This office in a kitchen belongs
to the design duo Nipa Doshi
and Jonathan Levien. White
walls and furniture create an
illusion of spaciousness and
enhance the decorative flashes
of bright scarlet.

Working with books

An old industrial building has been converted into a loft for the artist Edwina Sandys; note the arched brick ceiling and industrial fan. Lots of books have been introduced in plain white shelves, which, in turn, double up as a wall in the gallery space. The colourful textile, entitled *Literary Horse*, is one of the artist's own works.

▲ When Hugh Trevor-Roper (later Lord Dacre) was Master of Peterhouse College in Cambridge, his Aubusson carpet developed so many holes that old copies of *Country Life* were used to plug the gaps. Although the rest of the room was organized and elegant, the magazines added a touch of true English eccentricity.

◄ The desk as library: Sir Fitzroy Maclean's desk in his study at Strachur House in Scotland. All working writers are surrounded by reference books arranged in an order they alone understand.

▶ A fine example of warehouse chic: this is the former living-area and working studio of designers Nipa Doshi and Jonathan Levien, in London's East End. The industrial-style bookshelves are attached to the wall beside a plain work table and Eames *DSX* chairs. The school desk under the window came from a flea market.

Floor-to-ceiling bookshelves

Floor-to-ceiling bookcases are the answer for large, cold, unfriendly rooms (and many others besides). The sheer quantity and variety of the books take over the decor, meaning that neither pictures nor decorative objects are needed. Besides this, the wall of books provides insulation and improved acoustics. But the design needs to be carefully controlled. Do you want to reach the very top shelves? If so, you will need a ladder and a head for heights or, better still but more expensive (and perhaps requiring planning permission), a balcony running above door height but still allowing plenty of head room.

Then there is the layout of the shelves, which ideally should command more visual interest than simply running back and forth. For example, you could add a wider upright every metre or so, to create an effect of stacks; serry the books into shelves made like cubes; or, if your books are all different heights and widths, invest in breakfronts or asymmetric shelves. There's enjoyment to be had in designing a fancy cornice or pillars; or even putting a modern series of shelves into the grandest palatial room with putti and paintings, just for the contrast.

◄ Wooden cubes make up this floor-to-ceiling bookcase in Borja Azcarate's flat in Madrid. The monochrome scheme of walls, window and floor, with touches of dark tribal art, lends the room character and coherence.

▲ If books take over your life, it's surprising how much extra space can be found for them. The owner of this Provençal bastide slabs them from floor to ceiling and over the door.

This is a nineteenth-century
house in central London, built
specifically for an artist. A
serious book collector added the
two-tier library to the traditional
studio with its airy, deliberate,
cool light. The gallery of the
second tier provides reading-
space, leaving the ground floor
as a living-room.

In a Venetian palazzo, the
video artist Fabrizio Plessi has
designed his library with the
utmost good manners. The cube
bookshelves are intended to
merge into the background,
giving the ornate pilasters and
ceiling pride of place.

▲ Peter and Gillian Somerville-Large are both authors, and their eighteenth-century mill home in County Kilkenny, Ireland, is evidence of this. The bookshelves were made in the style of the period, with reeded uprights and frieze, by a local carpenter. Cards and prints are balanced against the background of books.

Overleaf: The bookshelves in this Victorian double drawing-room in a central London house have been ingeniously created to adapt to the varying height of the books while preserving a formal framework. Note how some of the short shelves are taller than others, and how the radiator in the centre is hidden by slatted woodwork. The whole is coloured in Farrow & Ball's 'Green Smoke' paint, a soft but strong colour.

▼ Strong sunlight can damage books over time, and diffused light is better for the reader, too. Here, once again, a monochrome scheme allows the books to make a major statement in the room. This is the contemporary country house, in Cape Town, of designer Stefan Antoni and architect Philip Olmesdahl.

▶ Three rooms are melded into one in designer Serena McCallum's long and narrow living-space. Library and dining-room meet in the foreground, while the living-area is at the rear.

Floor-to-ceiling bookshelves

Enclosed bookcases

There's no real need to enclose books behind wooden or glazed doors; they won't come to harm on open shelves. But the overall scheme of the room may be helped by reducing the impact of the books themselves and increasing the importance of the bookcases that hold them. Depending on the material used to enclose the books, they can be entirely hidden behind cupboard doors, or more clearly visible. Glass, with its reflections, is nearly as impenetrable as solid wood, while metal doors of various types, from vertical brass rails to frail chicken wire, allow the furniture to become the salient feature, rather than the books.

Enclosed bookcases are excellent if the room needs the symmetry that a pair of bookcases affords, and, if the shelves are to hold a variety of objects (not all of them beautiful), then enclosed wooden doors are the answer. Glass is fine in classical rooms, while chicken wire adds textural surface interest that distracts the eye from the books. Enclosed bookcases are also ideal for dining- and drawing-rooms, which do not need the scholarly approach of a formal library. Another bonus of such bookcases, and one I have used, is that obtrusive radiators can be hidden behind chicken wire or other open metal doors, allowing the heat to percolate without drawing attention to its source.

One way of ensuring a fine library is to buy the bookcases first and then find the house to suit them. This is exactly what the antiques dealer Will Fisher, of the London company Jamb Limited, did. This fine four-door bookcase, 3 metres (10 feet) high and 3.5 metres (11 feet) long, came from the British Museum and is made of brass and mahogany.

Working with books

◀ In the library of the country home – near Bedford, New York – of Stephen Sills and James Huniford, tall glass-fronted bookcases create an elegant effect and echo the long French windows and the display case containing a lobster. The spindly metal ladder, in its turn, mimics the lobster's jointed form.

▼ Sir Fitzroy Maclean's laden desk has already appeared (page 72). There are rather more formal arrangements for books in the Far Drawing Room of the same house, Strachur House, on Loch Fyne in Scotland. The two grandiose, pedimented bookcases, with glazed doors, stand symmetrically on either side of the marble fireplace.

▶ Formal bookcases with glazed doors suit the grand, empty spaces of Italian palazzi. Here, the white ceiling beams are echoed by the spare style of the built-in shelves. As this palazzo belongs to the Pucci family, the carpet, unsurprisingly, is abstract and colourful.

◄ Victorian town houses – this one is in the London district of Barnes – are ideal for the formal treatment of books. The reeded bookcase looks well beside the painted fireplace, dado rails and cupboard. The furniture and chandelier hark back to an eighteenth-century scheme.

▲ This is one corner of the library in the Tuscan palazzo belonging to the Marchesa Pucci. The sculptures add movement and a human touch to the highly formal arrangement of the books, while maintaining the Classical look of the room.

DESIGNING FOR BOOKS

Whether your books are for work or fun, it's important that they look good. To start with, make sure the depth and height of the shelves suit the books that you have. It's worth spending a lot of time considering how many small paperbacks and how many giant illustrated books need to be housed. Before you even think of calling in a joiner, decide carefully on the measurements between the shelves and from front to back (leaving a few centimetres or so of space above each book). Do not leave this to the joiner; he'll get it wrong.

Next, how many metres of shelving will you need (always allowing for expansion)? Will the shelves go from floor to ceiling or end with enough space below the latter to allow you to add a collection of busts or Greek vases (both popular in grand libraries)? Then there's lighting. It really must work so that not only can you see the titles on the books' spines, but also, the books can be lit up in an inviting way. This isn't easy, so it's worth getting an expert in to assess the type of lighting and advise on how to hide all the wiring. Do you want the shelves uplit, downlit, illuminated from the ceiling or with the bulbs hidden behind the books? This last method looks most effective as decor, but won't help much in reading the titles.

As well as built-in bookcases, which make a room into a library and can cut the room's size by more than half a metre (2 feet) in each direction, there's also the option of free-standing shelves. There are fine antique cabinets in mahogany or walnut with ormolu ornaments; painted and glazed free-standing cupboards; and eccentric modern shelves where the books do not stand upright but lean at crazy angles. These make a statement about the owner's interest in the work of designers (Ron Arad, Memphis, Philippe Starck) rather than suggesting much concern with the practicalities of storing books, but, in the right setting, they are stylish and witty.

I like the way books and objects can be juxtaposed on shelves. Carefully done, it doesn't suggest that you have shamefully run out of books, but that they are part of a display or collection. Like can be placed with like: Chinese vases beside books on Chinese art; model cars beside motoring books; and jewellery alongside biographies of Cartier and Chanel. Putting the two together allows an enquiring mind to see the display and then read about what is on show. Other parts of the shelves can be given cupboard doors – to hide the less reputable works.

Getting bookshelves exactly right is important. You should spend time on the preliminaries until the spaces are custom-made for your own library. Then it will be a constant pleasure for you.

Colours, materials and designs for bookshelves

It's hard to get away from the conventional configuration of bookshelves. Like chairs or baths, they have a specific job to do. However, within these rules, it's quite possible to come up with major variations. For a start, bookshelves don't need to be made of wood: metal is a common material, from industrial shelving to airy suspended shelves thin enough to have minimal impact. The shelves can be arranged in squares, cantilevered from the main structure or wall, or curved in circles like a dumb waiter.

The main uprights and horizontals may be wide and assertive, or neat and nearly invisible; they can be left as plain wood or steel, or coloured to match or contrast with their surroundings. The use of contrasting colours can make the shelves more important than their contents, or vice versa. In fact, there's a surprising number of decisions that need to be made in the design of apparently simple shelves.

The secret is to ensure that the shelves fit the style of the room – Classical, Baroque, minimalist, emphatic or unobtrusive. The room, therefore, will dictate the shelves' design, material and colour.

▶ A wall of books can be as decorative or discreet as you choose. The installation artist Fabrizio Plessi has opted for discretion in his palazzo flat in Venice.

▶ ◥ Adam Yarinsky's own weekend home in the Hudson valley north of New York is as uncompromising as the architect of the Architecture Research Office can devise. The wall of books on cantilevered shelves is designed to narrow and darken its space, revealing generous light beyond.

▶ ◢ Strictly disciplined, neat bookshelves are fitted into a tight corner of Dennis Dahlquist's small 1950s-style flat in Stockholm. The shelves include boxes, open planks and angled areas for displaying ceramics and books.

Chunky shelves of Brazilian
hardwood give a strong modern
emphasis to this traditional
apartment in Paris. The books are
shelved in co-ordinated groups –
either by similar bindings, or
by similar heights – separated by
large collections of ornaments.
The interior designer, Christophe
Pillet, restored the original
parquet floor and introduced
the hide lounging-chair.

The strong black-and-white pattern of the re-covered Eames chair dominates this near-monochrome scheme in the home of architect Haifa Hammani. The heavy shelves, with their cargo of colourful, variously stacked books, add a cheery touch and a hint of disorder to the room.

▲ The film producer David Puttnam's 'think tank' – a shed beside the water on his property in Ireland – uses a large bookcase as a room divider. In this kind of configuration, where double-sided bookcases are used, thought must be given to each side. Here, the shelves on the far side are blocked off.

◄ Dominique Picquier, a French textile designer, decided that a 1930s converted tool factory in Paris was the ideal showcase for her fabrics. A set of galvanized metal bookshelves fills up a bedroom.

▲ A circular bookcase – this one
is in mahogany – can be fitted
into a tight corner and, because
it swivels, will take plenty of
books. The painting in the room
beyond, *The Swimmers*, is by
Jean-Louis Germain.

◀ This room divider at
Yezmolaev, outside Moscow,
doubles the shelf space by having
rows of books on each side.
Standardized bindings help to
keep its appearance formal.

Free-standing and designer bookshelves

Generally, bookshelves are positioned with their backs to the wall, but this is not essential. Provided the structure is strongly made and the floor underneath able to bear the load, bookshelves can be constructed to spring from the wall, with only one side attached. This will, in effect, make a bay in the room. Or they can be entirely free-standing, usually in order to divide a large room into more manageable segments. Bookshelves as room dividers are effective: the area beyond is rendered virtually invisible, while light is still able to filter through. The little problem of displaying the books' pages on one side should be avoided by having the shelves made wide enough to hold two sets of books, one facing in each direction.

Completely free-standing bookshelves have different advantages: they can be taken around various rooms to suit changing decor and, when you move house, they can come with you. There are also elegant antique bookshelves – again mobile – that double up as consoles or chests with tops that provide generous space for display.

Designer bookshelves need to be chosen with care. The design should not detract from the bookcase's use (a frequent problem with work by today's celebrity designers, many of whom seem to prefer making statements to creating furniture). But, if the books can be happily put in and equally happily taken out, then a designer bookcase can be the focus of the room.

While preserving the sense of the past of this room, which was once a milking-parlour (see also page 89), the architect John Fell-Clark has added dynamism by using free-standing bookshelves to divide the living-room from the dining-area. The latter is furnished with chairs by Mies van der Rohe and a table that integrates a teak top with legs made of concrete pipes.

▼ This eccentric bookcase is the showpiece in Felicia Larsson's London loft. The space was converted by Norwegian architect Knut Hovland.

This is a corner of the panelled
drawing-room in the villa in
the Bois de Boulogne that
was the last home of the Duke
and Duchess of Windsor. It is
at once grand, because of the
elegant antiques and the decor
(by Boudin), and comfortable,
with domesticity provided by
family photographs and portraits
of dogs amid the formal
arrangement of the books.

▶ Early nineteenth-century bookcases, such as this one in lighting designer Charles Edward's country home in Northamptonshire, England, were designed to furnish corridors and halls.

◢ Writers always need books. These were owned by John Fowles and kept at his Regency villa overlooking the Cobb at Lyme Regis in Dorset, England. When he died he bequeathed the property to future generations of writers. Projecting the shelves into the room adds far more space than would be afforded by wall-mounted shelves.

▼ John Stefanidis designed this jauntily painted book tray for one of several libraries in his London house. It neatly holds a series of books for works in progress.

Low-level bookshelves

Storing books at ground level or at dado height is an excellent way of creating extra space in the cluttered library that is overfull of books, although it's not ideal for the regular reader, who has to kneel to read or reach the titles.

But if you are suffering from a serious book overload, this is a highly effective option: what else can you do with that metre (3 feet) or so under a large window? The shelves fill the gap between skirting and windowsill and, for neatness, should be designed to be the same depth as the sill above them. Low-level shelves also make a satisfactory room divider, solid but not too obtrusive, and because they are no more than a metre high, there's plenty of space above to give maximum light in the room while the lower half is made decoratively substantial with ranks of books.

Another advantage of low shelves is that plenty of wall space is left above them. This can be used for large paintings, hangings, groups of prints, sets of photographs or collections of small sculptures, glass or ceramics, either hung on the wall or casually exhibited leaning against it on the top of the shelves. Generally, low shelving is well mannered, allowing other displays more prominence.

Books have been ranged into a series of shelves to create a room divider in Lars Holbak's Copenhagen home. The antiques dealer and interior designer has kept the shelves low to allow lots of light in from the window and the garden beyond. Coloured glass vases catch and reflect the light.

▼ The owner of this tiny duplex in Dublin, Garrett O'Hagan, opened up the living-area and added a new, perforated-metal mezzanine at roof level. This has become a second sitting-area and a retreat.

▶ This double-height living-room at architect James d'Auria's home in the Hamptons is filled with light from many windows. The bookshelves are neatly hidden behind the sofas, and are further disguised by a set of leaning pictures balanced on their tops.

Designing for books

These low-level bookshelves are understated, thanks largely to the wall of windows above. This is at fashion designer Christina Kim's home in Los Angeles. She runs the clothing and housewares company Dosa.

Designing for books

This is a detail of one of the pair of bookshelves in James d'Auria's double-height living-room, shown on the previous pages. By painting the shelves to blend in with the wall and using pictures to decorate the tops, d'Auria has kept the shelves discreet.

Low-level bookshelves

Combining bookshelves with storage and display

One way to reduce the impact of full bookshelves is to allow open spaces where the volumes give way to artefacts. This needs to be handled with some care, in order to avoid the impression that there are not enough books in the house to fill a shelf. Heaven forbid.

I like the way some collectors mingle their reference works on, say, ancient Chinese ceramics, with actual examples of the ceramics themselves, carefully protected behind glass. Similarly, highly decorative objects, such as African masks, small sculptures and paintings, can be interspersed with relevant (or irrelevant) books. Any collector of such objects will undoubtedly have primed himself with a small library on his subjects. Other decorative pieces can simply be used for their looks and impact against the plain walls behind the shelves.

Books and their allied objects do not need to be on shelves; instead, they can be piled together on desks and tabletops. And, instead of being related by subject, they could be linked by appearance. Marbled bindings might vie with marble samples, gung-ho Victorian adventure books with medals and assegais, or children's stories with toys and teddy bears. It's great fun to make the matches.

In this apartment in the Barbican in London, the elegant rosewood set of shelves is a George Nelson original. In front stands a pair of Le Corbusier *Grand Confort* chairs from the QE2.

▲ An Eames lounge chair and ottoman are silhouetted against the bay window of architect Alex Michaelis's former drawing-room in London. Books are neatly arranged on discreet shelves.

◄ If you have a free-standing bed – as here, in the former apartment in London of interior designer John Wright – you can turn the headboard, also free-standing, into bookshelves and cupboards.

▶ Books stored both horizontally and vertically create interesting patterns, and are interspersed with lights and ornaments here in author Vivien Leone's former apartment at the top of New York's Gramercy Park Hotel.

▶▶ Designer Emma Wilson has made use of Moroccan building skills in her riad in Essaouira. The irregular shelves, holding magazines and artefacts as well as books, are built into the wall and plastered. Their deliberate plainness is offset by the pied cowhide table, which adds an exotic touch.

Designing for books

◀ In fashion designer Rosita Missoni's flat in Milan, a selection of beautifully bound books is mixed with family mementoes made by a friend.

▼ Anyone who collects books has to cope with ever-increasing stacks. This is Timothy Mawson's eighteenth-century garden-tour house and country store in New Preston, Connecticut, in which a collection of gardening books, tools, prints and old seed catalogues has clearly begun to take over.

▶ In this slightly eccentric arrangement, tureens, silhouetted against a dark background, are mixed with books stacked in various ways in a dresser in a corner of a Bermudian property.

Lighting

The decorative possibilities of books and bookcases can be greatly enhanced by clever lighting, and this should be considered along with the practicalities – always making sure that the lighting scheme is workable. You must be able both to find the books you need and to read them alongside the book stacks.

Basically, books and shelves can be downlit, which is generally practical, or uplit, which is less so. Downlighting can also turn a set of bookshelves into a colourful and decorative wall feature. Serious libraries may have two kinds of lighting: downlights in the ceiling or the tops of the shelves, and mobile Anglepoise-type lamps attached to the edge of the shelves. These allow beams to be moved to suit the reader.

More purely decorative schemes involve lights hidden at the back of the shelves, which turn the books into silhouetted blocks while producing a soft, diffused light. Perhaps this method is less helpful to serious readers, but it is good in some instances, for example, behind a bedhead, as it provides bedside lighting of a gentle nature. Similarly, lights can be introduced within the shelves, either behind opaque glass or as small table lamps. Again, this is more decorative than practical, but excellent where the bindings are as important as the content.

▶ A downlighter makes the titles easy to read as well as spotlighting the wall of books in designer Nina Campbell's former London home.

▶▶ A sliding blackboard door shuts off the children's rooms from the rest of Julian Powell-Tuck's London home. The architect has interspersed cubes of light with the books to illuminate a dark space.

LUST
for
wurds

IMMORTALIT

Individual directional spotlights
illuminate the books' spines as
well as adding interesting pools
of light. Here, bookcases lit in
this way flank a cupboard in a
Directoire French manor house.

◄ John Stefanidis is a designer who leaves nothing to chance. His London house is a series of library-cum-sitting-rooms in which books dominate the settings. When planning the rooms to house his huge collection of books, he worked out the spaces down to the last title.

▼ Splendid old books need special treatment. The books in these built-in shelves date from the thirteenth century and come from an old monastery. They are the focal point of this contemporary living-room designed by the architect Nico Rensch for a London mews house.

▲ The artist Suzy Murphy remade her nineteenth-century London house to bring as much light as possible into the rooms. Books are confined to niches on either side of the bed, while light-attracting unbleached linen covers both blinds and bedhead.

Trompe l'œil

While the notion of wallpaper made to look like the crammed shelves of a decorative library is a comparatively modern idea, the use of phoney books in a room goes back into history. Many historic libraries used real books in the shelves that were within easy reach, while piling the top and bottom areas with decorative spines that had no books behind them.

Similarly, the doors into a grand library might also be covered with book spines. While this makes it hard for the reader ever to find the way out of the room, continuity is assured. Well-bound, if dull, books were – and still are – offered for sale by the yard for just this purpose – although wallpaper is cheaper and easier to apply. Wallpaper, however, won't fool anyone for long, as the spines suspiciously repeat themselves. But pictures can be hung over the design, just as with more conventional wallpaper. The illusion of bookshelves will also change the perception of the room's size; it will seem bigger.

Another way to tackle *trompe l'œil* is to take a miscellaneous selection of books and cover each with matching paper (the cheap option) or have them bound in identical leather and buckram. This is one method of treating ugly or non-uniform bindings in order to achieve a homogeneous, minimal effect. Should the house lack books, as a last resort, any old second-hand titles can be bought very cheaply, covered and used to fill the shelves.

If you don't have the books, you can get the wallpaper. This one is 'Bibliothèque' by Brunschwig & Fils, used in Nina Campbell's former London home to disguise a jib door. I have also seen it used in a hotel lobby in San Francisco to make a tiny space seem friendlier.

Laurie Mallet's library in New
York has a whole series of real
books that she has treated with
resin so that they can't be
opened. A curious idea, but
an effective sculpture.

MAKING THE MOST OF BOOKS

Most of us who live and work with books never have enough space to keep them in order. The regular shelves get full to bursting, and more space must be found. But don't worry – there is always more space somewhere and, by the nature of books, what you do with them will form part of the decoration of a room. You do not even need bookshelves.

In the austere 1950s there was a craze for contemporary shelves consisting of good-looking wooden planks balanced on a series of plain bricks – and very nice they looked. But you can dispense with shelves altogether by just piling books up in a corner, on high dados around the room, or neatly balanced on sets of stairs. This by no means says 'untidy slob', but suggests you are a genuine absent-minded professor type. Book reviewers, who receive far more books than they need (but, conversely, hate to get rid of them), will pile them up in every room, occasionally with seriously deleterious consequences, although I've yet to hear of a critic being buried under his review copies. The piling method has its advantages – it costs nothing – but the disadvantage is that piles have to be moved aside every time you need a book from around the bottom of the heap.

At the opposite end of possible solutions to the bookshelving question is the face-out display, where the attractive dust jackets of some – or all – books are shown like pictures. If this is done with every book, the effect is more of a publisher's office than a home (maybe you like this idea), but choosing selective front covers creates the same impact as interspersing books with other objects. It also makes it easier to find what you need.

I don't know why coffee-table books are sometimes derided (why should I; I write them myself?). What's wrong with something beautiful and informative? What's more, I like them piled on low tables, inviting anyone to have a browse. Their size, weight and design mean that they are not really intended as page-turner reads but as something to dip into, in the search for good ideas. Leave such books lying about for a quick browse and you will find they produce all kinds of new and imaginative concepts.

The point about treating books in this casual fashion is that you are inviting people to read them. Piles of books on floors, stairs and tables are the very opposite from books behind glass in an intimidating library. You are saying that these books are valuable for what is in them, not because they are rare or first editions or valuable or impossibly scholarly. They do not need to be treated with kid gloves, but with warm hands and an open mind.

Books
without
bookshelves

People who really read books don't bother too much with storage systems, alphabetical order or tidy bookshelves. What they care about is books themselves, which generally are found lying all over the house, ready to be picked up for a quick paragraph or a somnolent read. Order and a system are for those who work with books and need, with the least possible delay, to find the exact reference source they have in mind.

That's not to say that readers, writers and researchers cannot be two-minded in their ways. The working library may be a paragon of order and logic; the books that are kept to read, on the other hand, will be in heaps, piles, baskets. Chaos and anarchy are the most descriptive words for this.

Any dedicated reader will constantly run out of shelf space; there may be plans to catch up but, meanwhile, books will find their way on to the stairs, into the glory holes and box rooms, will pile themselves up in bathrooms, on sofas and chairs and even under the bed or the dining-room table. There's nothing to be ashamed of in this. It's literary life.

◥ Even chairs can become temporary libraries. This pile on a loose-covered chair is in the drawing-room at Afra, a famous Corfu estate – mentioned several times in Edward Lear's diaries.

▶ Avid readers, such as journalist and designer Suzanne Boyd, need books in every room. This handy bedside stack is in her Manhattan apartment.

▶▶ A corridor and staircase in photographer Tim Beddow's French holiday home are papered with maps of Africa, a country he loves. Books are stacked on each of the wooden steps and an African mud cloth is slung over a rustic chair.

Books without bookshelves

▲▲ Books as sculpture: journalist Helen Kirwan-Taylor has a colourful pile sorted by size in her London living-room. Not suitable if there are tots or dogs around.

▲ Surprisingly, this heap of books is found in a home belonging to a former editor of South African *House & Garden* in the Little Karoo. His excuse is that he had no bookshelves and just piled the books against his bedroom wall. This room forms part of a converted pigsty.

▲ Designer Karen Roos has made sure that her tower of books conforms to the colours in her Swedish-style living-room in Cape Town. Books can easily be covered in heavy-duty paper to reduce or alter their impact.

◥ Albert Bang's seventeenth-century house in the South of France is full of the antiques dealer's 1930s furniture by Jean-Michel Franck. A small table-cum-stool by the fireplace is piled high with books, leaving people to shout round them.

Tables

The term 'coffee-table book' was originally and is still occasionally used as a sneering description, signifying the kind of book you put on display to aggrandize yourself, without ever bothering to read it. I've always thought this unfair: books should look beautiful, and heavily illustrated ones are designed to be sampled, rather than read zealously from cover to cover.

For that matter, coffee tables are eminently better suited to being piled with books than reduced to being empty spaces ready for that mid-morning cup of coffee (who ever has this today?). The same goes for even bigger tables. What is the point of keeping them empty when they will be greatly enlivened with a stack – or more – of amusing books? Books, chosen for their good looks as much as for their subject-matter, must be one of the easiest and cheapest ways of decorating a tabletop. No fragile porcelain or glass, but strong workaday books that can be dropped a dozen, and read many dozen, times.

Keep the books in careful piles, with the largest book at the base and the flimsiest at the top, so that they do not topple over and injure a passing dog; organize by edition, genre or colour to make them relevant to their surroundings, and books will surprise you by their decorative qualities.

▶ A round table, however makeshift, can be covered with floor-length fabric and made into a useful book repository. This one is in the bedroom of the Manhattan duplex belonging to an ex-curator of the Museum of Modern Art in New York, Joan Vass. Other informal arrangements of books are found in every room.

▶▶ The idea behind this chaotic series of books piled on a chunky table is that the owner, antiques dealer Albert Bang, can 'pull one out experimentally'. He does, of course, run the risk of an avalanche.

Making the most of books

▼ A long, low table stacked with books almost fills the width of Fabrizio Plessi's studio in a Venetian palazzo. No pile is too large to handle, and the light-filled room is otherwise left minimal in its effect.

▶ Bookcases in designer Muriel Brandolini's weekend home in the Hamptons have been designed by Andrea Branzi. A subfusc coffee table piled with books provides an island of calm in a sea of controlled colour. Walls, floor and furniture provide the strong hues of the room.

Making the most of books

▲ Books are stashed beside a large vase of tulips on a painted tray table. This is a neat splash of colour in Suzanne Boyd's Manhattan apartment.

▶ You might guess that this monstrous pile of books is found in the home of a professional reader. Note how all are presented with only the pages showing – not the titles. The house is in a village in Piedmont, Italy.

◥ Symmetrical piles of squared-off books convey a disciplined mind. These belong to Glen Senk and are on an eighteenth-century table in a Dutch Colonial house in Philadelphia. The 'abstract' behind the desk is in fact part of a cowshed floor.

Face-out display

In general, face-out display – where books are shown not with their spines but with their front covers outwards – is best kept for bookshops. But there are several exceptions to this rule.

One is if you are a collector of fine bindings, whether eighteenth- and nineteenth-century; first editions of Wodehouse or Evelyn Waugh; or those modern variations on craftsman bindings, such as the Folio Society adopts. If your enjoyment of books is in their binding rather than their content, then a face-out display is perfectly logical. The same would apply if you collect books by genre, such as Victorian novels, boys' own stories or modern photographic books where the front cover often features some marvellous shot by a Magnum photographer. Take pride in your front covers.

Another reason for face-out display is to help with sorting the books. You could make a book face outwards when a new subject appears on the shelf – gardening taking over from cookery, for example. The face-out volume will decoratively signal in the simplest way a change of subject.

A series of crumbling farm buildings in the Luberon was converted by the architect Jean-François Bodin into a contemporary-style hotel. He has used books – each displayed face out, its front cover carefully chosen – as a kind of wallpaper.

Simon Finch, a book dealer, had a crumbling property in west London converted into a home and gallery with the help of the architect Philip Meadowcroft. The books are displayed both by spine and face out.

Eccentric shelving

I'm generally not a great fan of designer shelving where the design genius has decided that classical shelving – proved over the generations – is boring. Like modern knives and forks, designer shelving too often ignores good sense and comfort. However, if the designer has managed to store books in a way that makes them easy to find and use, then there's nothing wrong with a bit of eccentricity. It may even be that, in their own way, modern designers are actually improving book storage.

It seems to me that the best innovative designs appear when the position of the shelves in a room needs some lateral thinking. Walls that are far from straight, buildings with circular walls, warehouses, barns and stables converted to houses, and such travelling homes as barges, Winnebagos and caravans, all demand new solutions to the problem of book storage. The shelves can cleverly allude to stable compartments, haylofts or poop decks; they can be designed to hold the volumes when travelling, or create significant features in huge, amorphous warehouse spaces.

But, above all, I think books should be treated with dignity and not merely as a design feature; if this is done, you will be safe.

▶ Ron Arad called his design for modern shelves *Bookworm*. This is shelving more interested in its effect than its use.

▶▶ This black-and-red lacquer workroom was designed by Claude Parent for a dramatic, structured effect.

Eccentric shelving

Gravity keeps these books in place. The backwards-slanting shelves are in a catamaran converted into a houseboat on the Thames at Battersea. Books do furnish a boat.

Making the most of books

► The Chinese architect and photographer Gao Bo also uses gravity to keep his books in place. He designed this unsettling set of shelves for his Modernist home in Beijing.

◢ A pair of newel posts salvaged from a derelict London studio has been extended to support the bookshelves – an idea worth copying. This is the sitting-room of a tiny cottage in Shropshire, which has been deliberately ruralized with second-hand furniture.

Using available space

There's virtually no corner of the house that cannot be made into an area for book storage. Faced with growing quantities of tomes, you will be surprised at the ingenuity you discover in yourself when it comes to finding extra space. The top metre or so (3 feet) of most rooms, for example, is rarely used, even for hanging pictures, so a shelf about 30 centimetres (1 foot) or more below the ceiling will accommodate several metres of – mostly unread – books. The same goes for low areas of rooms, such as the space underneath a windowsill. This, too, as discussed in the previous chapter, makes a good storage area that is rather more accessible than the space near the ceiling.

Even if you are hanging lots of pictures or have large pieces of furniture, there will be room corners, perhaps no more than 46 centimetres (18 inches) wide, which can be fitted with a series of bookshelves. Alcoves are useful, as are the areas on either side of a fireplace. Another idea is to use the space under the stairs, as long as it is not damp – for damp is a great danger to all books. All you need do is look around you and you will see plenty of unused space that can be piled, most decoratively, with your books.

◥ Neat piles of books with elegant bindings decorate a small shelf at the top of a narrow attic staircase in a chateau in Normandy belonging to antiques dealer Andrew Allfree, who is restoring it.

▶ Heywood Hill is a famous London bookshop (see also page 151) that does its best to look domestic. Here, books are ranged along the top of an eighteenth-century mantlepiece.

▶▶ The area under the stairs is always good for many feet of bookshelves – especially when the overarching staircase is as elegant as this one. It is in the interior designer Frédéric Méchiche's Paris apartment, in which the designer has sought to create a contrast between the traditional building and Modernist furnishings (see also page 24).

This minimalist scheme, in a London flat, has been deliberately upset by the disorderly way in which the books are shoved into the bookcase. As virtually all are arranged with their pale monochrome pages facing outwards, the arrangement resembles an abstract sculpture.

Making the most of books

Space above a bedroom
wardrobe has been fitted with
useful storage shelves for books.
For obvious reasons, however,
this area is unsuitable for regular
reference books.

► Everyone accumulates books that may be needed for reference only every few years, or some that have a sentimental value. The owner of this colonial house in Bermuda has used unwanted space high on the walls to house the archives.

▲ A bookcase was specially designed to fit this alcove in Timothy Mawson's Connecticut home. The curved middle shelves add charm to an otherwise simple design.

► Books can be hidden away in dark corridors and lit up only when in use. Gallery owner Gul Coskun has, sensibly enough, given pride of place to her six *Ulysses* etchings, created in 1935 by Matisse, and has let the books stay in the dark.

DIRECTORY

BOOKSHOPS AND SUPPLIERS

UK

The Aldeburgh Bookshop
42 High Street
Aldeburgh
Suffolk IP15 5AB
+44 (0)1728 452389
johnandmary@aldeburghbookshop.co.uk
aldeburghbookshop.co.uk

Established independent bookseller stocking new books. Administers the annual Aldeburgh Literary Festival.

Barter Books
Alnwick Station
Northumberland NE66 2NP
+44 (0)1665 604888
bb@barterbooks.co.uk
barterbooks.co.uk

One of the largest second-hand bookshops in the UK.

Bernard Quaritch Ltd
8 Lower John Street
Golden Square
London W1F 9AU
+44 (0)20 7734 2983
rarebooks@quaritch.com
quaritch.com

Founded in 1847; deals in rare books and manuscripts in many fields. The company also has an in-house bindery and undertakes conservation and restoration work.

Bertram Rota Ltd
31 Long Acre
London WC2E 9LT
+44 (0)20 7836 0723
bertramrota@compuserve.com
bertramrota.co.uk

Modern first editions, private press and artists' books, architecture and the applied arts, archives and manuscripts. Will carry out valuations, and purchase single books or collections of importance, or entire libraries. Provides advice and assistance with forming collections, throughout the world and to the precise requirements of clients in their particular areas of interest.

Bookartbookshop
17 Pitfield Street
London N1 6HB
+44 (0)20 7608 1333
info@bookartbookshop.com
bookartbookshop.com

Features the publications of some of Britain's best-known artist presses and publishers of artists' books, as well as books from abroad. The shop is a centre for individual and institutional collectors, artists, publishers and the aesthetically and bibliographically curious.

Browsers Bookshop and Café
60 The Thoroughfare
Woodbridge
Suffolk IP12 1AL
+44 (0)1394 388890
info@browsersbookshop.com
browsersbookshop.com

Independent bookshop selling new books; runs a separate children's bookshop a few doors down from the main shop:

Young Browsers
33 The Thoroughfare
Woodbridge
Suffolk IP12 1AH
+44 (0)1394 382832

Daunt Books
83 Marylebone High Street
London W1U 4QW
+44 (0)20 7224 2295
marylebone@dauntbooks.co.uk
dauntbooks.co.uk

New and second-hand books on a wide variety of subjects. Specialists in travel literature and fine writing of most genres. Other branches at Belsize Park, Chelsea, Hampstead and Holland Park.

Golden Books Group
Blurridge Farm
Ridge Hill
Combe Martin
Devon EX34 0NR
+44 (0)1271 883204
goldenbooksgroup.co.uk

Professional buyers and sellers of fine-quality leather-bound books. A valuable source of information about rare books and library accessories.

Hay Cinema Bookshop
Castle Street
Hay-on-Wye
near Hereford HR3 5DF
+44 (0)1497 820071
sales@haycinemabookshop.co.uk

The longest-established of the big bookshops in Hay. A huge range of stock: up to 200,000 volumes on all subjects.

Heywood Hill Ltd
10 Curzon Street
London W1J 5HH
+44 (0)20 7629 0647

Antiquarian and children's books.

Judd Books
82 Marchmont Street
London WC1N 1AG
+44 (0)20 7387 5333
juddbooks.com

Very large stock of used, remaindered and academic books, especially on architecture, history and philosophy.

Maggs Bros Rare Books
50 Berkeley Square
London W1J 5BA
+44 (0)20 7493 7160
+44 (0)20 7518 9530
enquiries@maggs.com
maggs.com

Established in 1853; one of the world's largest antiquarian booksellers. Buys and sells, worldwide, books and manuscripts of the highest quality, and staff act as advisors and booksellers to many of the world's finest collections. Also stocks books over a wide price range, and has expertise in shipping books all over the world.

Review
131 Bellenden Road
Peckham
London SE15 4QY
+44 (0)20 7639 7400
review@btconnect.com
reviewbookshop.co.uk.

Small shop with an excellent selection of new titles; very much part of the local community.

Travis & Emery Books on Music
17 Cecil Court
London WC2N 4EZ
+44 (0)20 7240 2129
enquiries@travis-and-emery.com
travis-and-emery.com

New and old books on music; second-hand and antiquarian music; opera programmes; prints and photographs; playbills; libretti.

US

Antiquarian Booksellers' Association of America
20 West 44th Street
Fourth Floor
New York, NY 10035–6604
+1 212 944 8291
hq@abaa.org
abaa.org

Berkshire Books
2 Park Row
Chatham, NY 12037
+1 518 392 2052
berkbooks@taconic.net
berkshirebooks.net

Second-hand book dealers.

Worldwide

AbeBooks Inc.
Suite 500, 655 Tyee Road
Victoria, BC
V9A 6X5
Canada
abebooks.com

AbeBooks is an online marketplace for books. More than 110 million new, used, rare and out-of-print books are offered for sale through the AbeBooks website from thousands of booksellers around the world.

BOOKBINDERS, RESTORERS AND FINE BOOK PRESSES

Australia

Queensland Bookbinders' Guild Inc.
P.O. Box 3009
Tarragindi
QLD 4121
qbg.org.au

Victorian Bookbinders' Guild Inc.
P.O. Box 151
Bulleen
VIC 3105
info@tomorrowsgraphics.com.au
avoca.vicnet.net.au

Canada

Association des relieurs du Québec
C.P. 1196 succursale Desjardins
Montréal, QC
H5B 1C3
relieursduquebec.ca

Canadian Bookbinders and Book Artists Guild
60 Atlantic Avenue
Suite 112
Toronto, ON
M6K 1X9
+1 416 581 1071
cbbag@cbbag.ca
cbbag.ca

Hélène Francœur
3064 ave St-Samuel
Québec, QC
G1C 3T2
+1 418 640 7303
info@hfrancœur.com
hfrancœur.com

Award-winning bookbinder: binding design, bookbinding, restoration, decorated papers, fine press printing.

Robert Wu
+1 416 927 1367
robert@studiorobertwu.com
studiorobertwu.com

Designer bookbinder and marbler in Toronto; operates a small bindery and marbling factory from home under the name Studio Robert Wu. Specializes in miniature bindings.

UK

Book Works
19 Holywell Row
London EC2A 4JB
+44 (0)20 7247 2203
mail@bookworks.org.uk
bookworks.org.uk

Contemporary visual-arts publisher with an international reputation for commissioning, publishing and promoting contemporary artists' books. Activities include bookbinding; box-making; portfolios; letterpress printing; designers' prototypes; presentation.

Croft Printers & Bookbinders Ltd
Unit 3
Kangley Business Centre
Kangley Bridge Road
London SE26 5BW
+44 (0)20 8659 4224

Designer Bookbinders, UK
membership@designerbookbinders.org.uk
designerbookbinders.org.uk

One of the foremost societies devoted to the craft of fine bookbinding. Promotes, maintains and improves standards of design and craft in hand bookbinding. Its membership includes some of the most highly regarded makers in the fields of fine bookbinding, book arts and artists' books. For details, contact the Membership Secretary.

The Fleece Press
95 Denby Lane
Upper Denby
Huddersfield HD8 8TZ
+44 (0)1226 792200
simon@fleecepress.com
fleecepress.com

Private printing press and publisher, owned and run by Simon Lawrence, producing limited editions of hand-made books using the letterpress method, usually illustrated by, or about, wood engravers and printmakers.

Ludlow Bookbinders Ltd
Unit 8, Lower Barns Business Park
Ludford
Ludlow
Shropshire SY8 4DS
+44 (0)1584 878110
info@ludlowbookbinders.co.uk
ludlowbookbinders.co.uk

Produces a wide range of books and bespoke goods tailored to the customer's requirements. Binding services, rebinds, special packaging, private press work.

Philip Smith
philipsmithbookart@tiscali.co.uk

Book-art making. His work is represented in many public and private collections throughout the world.

Shepherds Bookbinders Ltd (formerly Falkiner Fine Papers)
76 Rochester Row
London SW1P 1JU
+44 (0)20 7630 5323
bookbinding.co.uk

also at
76 Southampton Row
London WC1B 4AR
+44 (0)20 7831 1151

Includes a hand-bindery, specializing principally in fine leather binding. Traditional techniques and materials are used, but there is also a creative workshop experimenting with new design concepts. A bespoke binding service, and conservation and restoration services, are also available.

The Society of Bookbinders, UK
info@societyofbookbinders.com

The Society of Bookbinders is dedicated to traditional bookbinding and to the preservation and conservation of the printed and written word.

Trevor Lloyd
Hand bookbinder and book restorer
12 Old Street
Ludlow
Shropshire SY8 1NP
+44 (0)1584 876565
info@trevorlloyd.co.uk
trevorlloyd.co.uk

Binds and restores antiquarian books for book collectors, dealers and private libraries. He is able to restore books to the exact style of their period and country of origin.

Victoria Hall Hand Decorated Papers
The Old Stores
32 Magpie Road
Norwich
Norfolk NR3 1JQ
+44 (0)1603 764411
victoria@hall1120.fsbusiness.co.uk

Marbled and paste papers from stock in eighteenth- and nineteenth-century styles suitable for book restoration. Welcomes custom orders in original and contemporary designs for new publications or fine-press books.

US

Guild of Book Workers
521 Fifth Avenue
New York, NY 10175–0083
+1 212 757 6454
cool-palimpsest.stanford.edu

The national organization for all the book arts.

Jack & Taff Fitterer
432 Big Brook Road
Indian Lake, NY 12842
fitterer@acmenet.net

Superb workmanship.

BOOKPLATE DESIGNERS

Australia

New Australian Bookplate Society
stoplaughing.com.au/bookplatesociety

For more information, contact
the President:
m.ferson@unsw.edu.au

Germany

Exlibris – insel.de
Klaus Kampe
Schmiedehof 15
D–10965 Berlin
+49 30 440 48 232
exlibris–1 a.de

UK

The Bookplate Society
11 Nella Road
London W6 9PB
bookplatesociety.org

International society of collectors,
bibliophiles, artists and others dedicated
to promoting bookplate study. The website
provides contact details of many expert
designers in the field.

US

American Society of Bookplate
Collectors and Designers (ASBC&D)
exlibrisusa@hotmail.com
bookplate.org

Formed to further the study, collecting
and development of bookplates. The
ASBC&D maintains a current list of
names and addresses for ex-libris
artists from all countries, and a
catalogue of hundreds of sample
designs by international artists
is available.

Bookplate Ink
P.O. Box 547577
Orlando, FL 32854
info@bookplateink.com
bookplateink.com

Bookplates.com
info@bookplates.com

Supplier of fine traditional bookplates.
Using the interactive custom-design
interface, the customer chooses the
bookplate design, quantity, ex-libris
message, text and formatting. Each
set is then prepared by a professional
graphic designer, and printed using
offset lithography and materials of
archival quality.

LIGHTING

UK

The Great British Lighting Company
Denham Way
Fleetwood
Lancashire FY7 7PR
+44 (0)1253 873503
greatbritishlighting.co.uk

Global lighting manufacturer with more
than 100 years' experience. Has a large
range of traditional and contemporary
lighting, and can design, restore or
reproduce lighting to the customer's
exact specification, matching lighting
from the last century and beyond,
using the latest technology.

John Cullen Lighting
561–563 King's Road
London SW6 2EB
+44 (0)20 7371 5400
design@johncullen.co.uk
sales@johncullen.co.uk
johncullenlighting.co.uk

Offers a complete design service for all
aspects of interior and exterior lighting,
whether contemporary or traditional.
Sells a unique collection of light fittings.
Showroom displays many different
designs, products and effects. Full
brochure available on the website.

LIBRARY FURNITURE

BOOKCASES AND SHELVING

UK

Arthur Brett and Sons Ltd
103 Pimlico Road
London SW1W 8PH
+44 (0)20 7730 7304
pimlico@arthur-brett.com
arthurbrett.com

Designs and handcrafts fine traditional
English furniture.

David Salmon Bespoke Furniture
Hoory Vaseghi
1/19 Chelsea Harbour Design Centre
London SW10 0XE
+44 (0)20 7349 7575
sales@davidsalmon.com
USA enquiries:
ussales@davidsalmon.com
davidsalmon.com

Designers and manufacturers of hand-
made, classic, museum-quality furniture.
Also create bespoke pieces made to
individual specification.

US

Jack Frederick Modern Furniture
116 E. Moreland Avenue
Philadelphia, PA 191118
+1 215 248 4144
info@jackfrederick.com
jackfrederick.com

Dynamically designed and unusual
modern bookcases, desks and chairs
for the study, library or office.

Levenger
levenger.com

Suppliers of fine accessories and
furniture for the study or library.

STEPS AND LADDERS

US

Putnam Rolling Ladder Co., Inc.
32 Howard Street
New York, NY 10013
+1 212 226 5147
info@putnamrollingladder.com
putnamrollingladder.com

Manufactures standard and custom rolling ladders for libraries and commercial and residential use. Also makes trestle ladders, step stools, pulpit and industrial steel ladders.

LIBRARY ACCESSORIES

UK

The Bodleian Library Shop Online
shop.bodley.ox.ac.uk

Bookplates, library accessories, stationery and some library furniture.

Bonhams
The Gentleman's Library Sale
bonhams.com/gentlemanslibrary

The sale features traditional library furniture, including desks, writing-tables and bookcases, complemented by selected scientific instruments, marine and other models, globes, desk accessories and curiosities.

The British Library
96 Euston Road
London NW1 2DB
+44 (0)870 444 1500
shop.bl.uk

The shop stocks a small amount of accessories and stationery, including bookends, for the study or library. Also a wide variety of books, many of which are related to holdings in the library.

OKA Direct Ltd
Unit 3A
Vogue Industrial Park
Tower Road
Berinsfield
Oxfordshire OX10 7LN
0844 815 7380
or from outside UK: (+44) 1865 342 300
customerservice@okadirect.com
okadirect.com

Mail-order company that also has a number of shops in the south of England. Supplies a range of products, including desk accessories, lamps, wall lights and library steps.

US

Gaylord Brothers
gaylord.com

Supplies pre-cut book covers in different sizes to protect books. Also stocks bookcases, other library furniture and storage boxes.

The Thomas Jefferson Visitor Center and Smith Education Center Monticello Museum Shop
monticello.org
monticellostores.stores.yahoo.net

Considerable collection of study and library accessories and reproduction library furniture.

ARCHITECTS

These are the practices that produced the designs for libraries that appear on pages 2, 6–7, 9, 11 and 12.

Gianni Botsford Architects
83–84 Berwick Street
London W1F 8TS
+44 (0)20 7434 2277
giannibotsford.com

Peter L. Gluck & Partners
646 West 131st Street
New York, NY 10027
+1 212 690 4950
gluckpartners.com

Timothy Hatton Architects
139 Freston Road
London W10 5BU
+44 (0)20 7727 3484
thal.co.uk

Trout Studios
227 Turkey Drive
Dripping Springs, TX 78620
+1 512 894 0774
troutstudios.com

ADDITIONAL INFORMATION

Firsts Magazine
firsts.com
Published ten times a year. Offers a wealth of information for the book collector.

INDEX

Page numbers in *italic* refer to the illustrations

ACKNOWLEDGEMENTS/ PICTURE CREDITS

The publisher gratefully acknowledges the kind and expert assistance of Karen Howes and her photographic agency, The Interior Archive. All the images reproduced in the book were supplied by The Interior Archive, with the exception of those on pages 2, 6–7, 9, 11 and 12 (see list below for details).

From The Interior Archive:
Bill Batten: p. 140
Tim Beddow: back jacket, pp. 18t, 31t, 46–47, 49, 55, 58–59, 81, 104, 117bl, 123, 127, 129, 131, 141b, 150, 156
Tim Clinch: p. 74l and r
Jacques Dirand: pp. 20–21
Miguel Flores Vianna: pp. 65t, 90–91
Vincent Knapp: p. 139
Mark Luscombe-Whyte: front jacket, back jacket, pp. 24, 26l, 30, 31bl, 50, 60, 65b, 68t, 89, 93t, 94, 96t, 98–99, 105, 107, 108–109, 109t, 133tl and br, 134–35, 136–37, 143, 149, 153
Eduardo Munoz: back jacket, p. 138
Ianthe Ruthven: p. 77
Christopher Simon Sykes: back jacket, pp. 26r, 28–29, 32–33, 36–37, 38, 38–39, 44, 45l and r, 48–49, 51, 52, 66–67, 70–71, 72b, 85b, 110, 113t and b, 114, 118–19, 120–21, 130, 142b, 146l, 147
Simon Upton: back jacket, pp. 16–17, 18b, 22t and b, 22–23, 23t, 25, 31br, 34t, 39, 40–41, 52–53, 53, 56–57, 61tl and b, 62, 63, 64–65, 69, 73, 76, 82–83, 84, 85t, 86, 87, 92–93, 101t and br, 102–103, 109b, 115, 124–25, 126b, 128t, 132, 133tr and bl, 141t, 142t, 144, 146r, 155
Edina van der Wyck: pp. 15, 27, 78–79, 96b, 106, 112
Fritz von der Schulenburg: back jacket, pp. 19, 23bl and r, 34b, 35, 41, 42–43, 61tr, 68b, 72t, 75, 80, 96–97, 97, 100, 101bl, 116, 117t and br, 126r, 128b, 128–29, 145
Jakob Wastberg: p. 93b
Luke White: back jacket, pp. 95, 99, 111

Other picture credits:
Paul Hester, Hester & Hardaway: pp. 11, 12
Christian Richters: back jacket, p. 9
VIEW Pictures/Peter Cook: p. 2
Paul Warchol Photography: pp. 6–7

DIVIDER ILLUSTRATIONS

p. 2: Architect Timothy Hatton was commissioned by a 'polymath collector' to add two storeys to the top of a seventeenth-century London town house. The new space includes a double-height library with its own mezzanine gallery and additional study. The library, which is top-lit by three skylights and lined on three sides with continuous bookshelves made of white plaster, doubles as a family sitting-room.

pp. 6–7: Peter Gluck, an architect, designed a 'scholar's library' for his wife, Carol, who is a writer and academic. Conceived as a separate, new building, it is located in the Hudson Valley, upstate New York, close to where the family have a country home. The dramatic Modernist cube, surrounded by woods, comprises an upper storey – which is a work space furnished with a desk and shelves for books that are in use – and a lower level with extensive storage space. Would-be clients are queueing up for something similar.

pp. 16–17: Detail of a bookshelf in the London studio – on the top floor of an old commercial building in Covent Garden – of fashion designer Paul Smith. His ideas are stimulated when surrounded by clutter, music and conversation.

pp. 56–57: Shelves that form part of the writing-room in the late author John Fowles's home in Lyme Regis, Dorset, England. The room houses a great library, comprising half fiction, half natural history books. Although these shelves look orderly enough, on others the books jostle with a jumbled array of fossils, bones, animal skulls and Syrian statues.

pp. 90–91: Designer Asli Tunca and her sculptor husband, Carl Vercauteren, used panels of old chestnut in their Istanbul town house. The books and files on the shelves are covered in goatskin parchment and lettered by hand.

pp. 124–25: Designer Ilse Crawford used a shelf to display her favourite books and other collectibles in her former London apartment.

p. 149: Bright colours make sense in architect Richard Legorreta's Mexican home, where the quality of light enhances them. The room is skilfully designed to maximize the shelving without making the area oppressive.

p. 150: If you no longer need your library ladder, turn it into more shelves. This one is stacked at the entrance to Marie-France Brown's drawing-room in her Gascon farmhouse.

p. 155: The floor of Glen Senk's and Keith Johnson's library is, like many in the house, painted ebony to create a studious and snug room. The house is just outside Philadelphia.

p. 156: Old bindings, well-worn and well-used, have a beauty of their own.

First published 2009 by

Merrell Publishers Limited
81 Southwark Street
London SE1 0HX

merrellpublishers.com

British Library Cataloguing-in-Publication Data:
Geddes-Brown, Leslie.
Books do furnish a room.
1. Books in interior decoration.
I. Title
747.9-dc22

ISBN 978-1-8589-4491-3

Produced by Merrell Publishers Limited
Designed by Paul Arnot
Project-managed by Lucy Smith
Indexed by Hilary Bird

Printed and bound in China

Front jacket: photograph by Mark Luscombe-Whyte (see page 60)

Back jacket: photographs by (top row, left to right): Fritz von
der Schulenburg (see page 41); Christopher Simon Sykes
(see pages 32–33); Christian Richters (see page 9); Simon Upton
(see page 63); (middle row, left to right): Tim Beddow (see page 55);
Christopher Simon Sykes (see pages 70–71); Eduardo Munoz
(see page 138); Christopher Simon Sykes (see pages 120–21);
(bottom row, left to right): Mark Luscombe-Whyte (see page 143);
Tim Beddow (see page 127); Luke White (see page 99); Simon
Upton (see page 61)